What People Are Saying About
Discover Your Next Best Step:
10 Proven Principles
of Servant LeaderShip Wisdom

"When I first received this book, I picked it up with the idea of giving it a quick overview ... I couldn't put it down until I'd devoured the entire thing! I love the way Gord integrated his strong faith and rich business experience into an inspiring, engaging process that challenges me to "discover my next best step."

—Don Adams, owner, Dale Carnegie - Chicago

"Gordon Bell, my friend and mentor, has been a leader and thought leader most of his life. Leading successful businesses and mentoring successful business leaders has always seemed natural to him. What few people know is that Gordon is a lifelong learner, pressing for the principles that lift people and organizations to success and significance. You will be doing yourself, your family and the organizations you lead a favor by reading this book and adopting its well-proven principles."

—Al Caperna, husband and father;
chairman CMC Group; director C2Bevents

"My lifetime friend, Gordon Bell, has walked the narrow path that has led him to become a passionate and effective servant leader. Along the journey, he has discovered 10 proven principles that can guide his readers to fulfill their desire to be the leader that Christ has called them to be."

—Dan Coats, United States Senator for Indiana

"Having known Gordon for a few years, I can honestly say he overflows with wisdom! God has used him to encourage me, and hundreds of other leaders, to seek God's will in every decision we make. This book is a wonderful tool for every servant leader!"

—Patrick Fischl, middle school pastor,
The Chapel - Fort Wayne, Indiana

"Discover Your Next Best Step" does a masterful job of inspiring and motivating. Using scripture as a foundation and supplemented by real life examples, each chapter gave me ideas to use and information to share. The tools are good for leaders in the workplace and throughout their communities. It will bring joy, laughter and even tears as you read!"

—Cordia Harrington, CEO, *The BunLady*, The Bakery Cos.

"I have had the privilege of being a part of focus groups that have previewed this material. It has a proven record of effectiveness for business, not-for-profit and faith-based organization leadership. Bell gives us a text that is both simple and profound. He also gives us a context for each of the principles through case studies from his years of experience in leading major corporations."

—Rick Hawks, lead pastor, The Chapel - Fort Wayne, Indiana

"Having spent years mastering the skills of leadership from the ground floor up, Gordon Bell has now condensed his life lessons into one succinct, very readable book. Profit from this guidance and wisdom."

—Dr. Dennis E. Hensley, author, *Jesus in the 9 to 5*

"Gordon Bell is a no nonsense business mind with a heart for God. He sees no conflict between building great and lasting companies while applying biblical principles at every step. This is refreshing and important, and frankly, quite rare. Read this book, better yet apply it to both life and work."

—Ambassador J. Douglas Holladay,
former diplomat and investment banker

"Gordon shares timeless truths that continue to transform his business and his life by serving every person he encounters. You will be forever impacted from reading this book."

—Mitch Kruse, author, *Restoration Road*

"My friend Gord has taken his years of experience, his failures and successes, and written a book that will speak to everyone, no matter their age or vocation. Why? Because it is based on Principles … not philosophy, not methods, and not Gordon's ideas – although you will gain some great insights from his vast experience. This book is Principle-based, bathed in scripture, and true wisdom. If you apply what you read in *Discover Your Next Best Step,* you will witness a change in your own heart which in turn will help those you encounter each day as you journey through life.
Well done, my friend."

—Larry Lance, executive director,
Fort Wayne Youth for Christ

"Too busy to bring more meaning into your life? If you read Gordon Bell's newest book, *Discover Your Next Best Step: 10 Proven Principles of Servant LeaderShip Wisdom,* you'll see that

Gordon's story is not only profound and heartfelt, but also truly restorative. Gordon's questions touch your soul. Read how a busy executive changed his life, and the lives of many others, with his strong belief in God's purpose for each of us."

—Louise O'Sullivan, CEO, Prime Advantage

DISCOVER YOUR

NEXT BEST

10 PROVEN PRINCIPLES OF SERVANT LEADERSHIP WISDOM

STEP

GORDON D. BELL

DISCOVER YOUR NEXT BEST STEP:
10 PROVEN PRINCIPLES OF SERVANT LEADERSHIP WISDOM

ISBN 978-0-9974078-1-5

Library of Congress Control Number: 2016937058

Lake Effect Press
993 Chestnut Hills Parkway
Fort Wayne, IN 46814
(260) 625-5595

Printed in the United States of America
10 9 8 7 6 5 4 3 2

To my wife, Pat, and my sons, Jim and Matt.
I love you.

Acknowledgements

I would like to extend my heartfelt thanks to those who contributed to the writing of this book. This would not have been possible without you.

Mitch Kruse – Thank you for an early and long-lasting friendship. Our insightful discussion on Restoration Road prompted me to seek an even deeper understanding of the 10 principles outlined in this book, and for that, I am truly grateful.

Dennis Hensley – Thank you for your support and for encouraging me to pursue publication. Your insight into the world of publishing and your oversight have been invaluable.

My wife Pat – Thank you for being a constant source of encouragement throughout this process. I value your perspective, and I am humbled by your love and support.

Jennifer Bell – Thank you for listening, transcribing, offering opinions, revising, and staying the course.

Pam Musick – Thank you for guiding the development of the learning techniques and discussion questions throughout the book.

Marilyn Miller – Thank you for being a day-to-day administrator of the Midland business and for contributing to the learning questions and tools.

The Chapel – Thank you for providing an environment for me to present the 10 principles to more than 30 men in your bible study group. Thank you to Rick Hawks for your support and guidance. Thank you to Patrick Fischl for allowing me to teach a servant leadership program for middle school students.

Finally, thank you to the many pastors, Sunday School teachers, professors, colleagues, and friends who have made an impact on my life. You have challenged me to grow, and now, I hope to inspire others to do the same.

Table of Contents

About the Author

Gordon Bell is a lifelong businessman who has established himself as a trusted mentor and coach. Throughout the years he has become one of the region's go-to thought leaders in the business sector. He cherishes the opportunity to serve other business owners through his role as president of The Midland Group, a highly-regarded business advisory firm located in Fort Wayne, Indiana.

On the job and off, Gordon is passionate about developing meaningful relationships. The lessons he's learned from business colleagues, fellow Christ-followers, family and friends have been instrumental in the development of the principles you will read about in this book. Shared experiences with others truly warm Gordon's heart, and he routinely strives to develop a better understanding of spiritual truths through his interactions with others.

Gordon and his wife, Pat, have been married for nearly 50 years. They have two sons, two daughters-in-law and nine grandchildren. On summer weekends Pat and Gord love to escape to their home-away-from-home in Saugatuck,

Michigan. There, they enjoy the relaxing pace of life on Lake Michigan.

For more information about Gordon Bell and The Midland Group, go to themidlandgroup.net.

Foreword

by Mitch Kruse

I met Gordon Bell when I was 24 years old, and he was consulting a mutual friend who was running for our district's Congressional seat. I was immediately engaged by Gordon's charisma. Fast forward two decades, and I received an email from Gord asking to reconnect. He had just watched one of my television programs where I teach the Bible through stories of restoration in order to connect culture with Christ. We scheduled a late-morning appointment for hot chocolate.

God was moving in Gord, something I learned to be a common occurrence in his life. We connected on so many levels during our hot chocolate that we decided to keep talking at a nearby restaurant where we had lunch. I didn't want the conversation to end. Gord understood me and spoke so much wisdom into my life. We scheduled another appointment, and we've been getting together regularly ever since.

Gordon Bell's 10 proven servant leadership principles have guided him through the peaks and valleys of his incredible life. Whether you are a student, a professional athlete, a busy wife and mother managing her household, a business owner, a nonprofit leader, a trade professional, a marketplace executive, a coach, a teacher, or a ministry volunteer, Gordon Bell understands you, and he will help you discover your **Next Best Step**. You won't want your conversation with him to end.

Preface

Put Your Boots On

More than 20 years ago, after being a hard-charging executive with a couple of companies for the better part of two decades, I found myself without a job. The company I'd been working for was in the hands of new management, and suddenly, I realized I was going to have to start over.

That Sunday my wife Pat and I went to church. Dr. Wes Gerig was the interim pastor at First Missionary Church, and his sermon that day was about Nehemiah and how he had developed a plan to rebuild the walls of Jerusalem. I wept through the entire sermon. Like Nehemiah, I knew I needed to rebuild, too. After the service I met with Dr. Gerig and told him what had happened with my job, and he kindly shared some heartfelt words of encouragement and God's wisdom.

Monday was even harder. The realization that I had nowhere to go was unnatural. As we woke up, Pat issued a challenge.

"Are you going to stay in bed or put your boots on?" she asked with her incredible insight and grace.

> **"For I know the plans I have for you," declares the Lord, "plans to prosper you and not to harm you, plans to give you hope and a future.**
>
> **Jeremiah 29:11, NIV**

I didn't even think about it. I got out of bed, showered and dressed in a shirt and tie. I headed into my home office and began spinning the old Rolodex. I contacted all of the wonderful people who had served me well throughout the years.

Six days later I received a letter from my father-in-law, Jim. He always had a way of coming up with the best advice when I least expected it. Here's an excerpt from his letter:

> Regarding the things we cannot alter. GOD gave life, we can assuredly trust Him for lesser things too. Commit all your anxieties to Him today. Allow a little slack in the rope, rest at anchor, say a prayer of thanksgiving, and sit back and await the answer which I know will be provided.

Within a few days, I was having lunch with a longtime friend and business colleague. He extended an invitation. "Come work out of my office. You can have access to the phones and staff -- anything you need. Not only that, I invite you to attend our staff meetings."

Initially, I wasn't sure what to do, but my wife encouraged me to consider the opportunity. "Do it," she said. "It's a gift."

I didn't realize it at the time, but by giving me a place to go, my colleague had given me a sense of purpose. This was God working through my friend, who had been granted a similar favor in his past.

During the next three months, as I met with many friends and colleagues in the Fort Wayne area, I began to see that God was revealing my purpose. Some of these people had been in my life for years. Others I had just met. My goal at the time was to figure out what God wanted me to do and see how it aligned with my gifts and talents. I would document notes after each meeting, prayerfully considering what God might be doing in my life.

I explored numerous opportunities, trying to figure out how I might glorify God. I interviewed to be a college president, and I thought about delving into management roles in other industries. I even spoke with our senator, a longtime friend, and considered running his campaign. Looking back, God was slowing me down and giving me an opportunity to listen to Him through others. I was blessed, thanks to the insight and forethought of my attorney, to have the time and resources needed to explore my **Next Best Step**. Did I want to be a CEO? I didn't think so. Instead, I was being called to be a servant leader to other CEOs, possibly serving as their coach and mentor. I started a company during that recessionary period called Bell International that allowed me to provide advisory services to at least a dozen companies in crisis or transition.

Throughout the years, my work has changed -- but my desire to be a servant leader has not.

I ultimately closed Bell International, and in the early 1990s, I acquired Midland Inc., with my longtime friend Jack. Midland Inc. was one of the oldest international import/export companies with origins dating back to World War I. It had offices in Fort Wayne, Belgium and Singapore, a marketing venture in France and a manufacturing license in Singapore. Jack and I added our unique touch to this well-established company, later creating Midland Partners.

In August 2000, The Midland Group was born out of Midland Partners. Today, it is a multi-state business enterprise, offering a variety of services, currently including Midland Management Solutions, Midland Private Equity Capital and Lake Effect Press. Truly, I have found my calling.

Strangely, all of this came after spending some considerable time in the valley, and I know that experience was a crucial part of the process. You see, each one of us spends time dealing with trials and hardships in life as we search for freedom and purpose. These valleys – and our ability eventually to work our way out of them – are opportunities for personal growth. They make us stronger, and they build a foundation for future success. It prepares us for discipleship and eternal life.

Next time you find yourself in the midst of a personal crisis, remember what my wife said to me: "You can stay in bed, or you can put your boots on." Get up and figure out your **Next Best Step**.

Servant LeaderShip Wisdom

YOU are called to be a leader.

Don't think so?

Consider this. If you have an employee, a colleague, a child, or a neighbor who is influenced and/or inspired by your words and actions, you are a leader. And, as you continue to develop your spheres of influence, you demonstrate LeaderShip skills.

I'm reminded of the episode of Jesus sleeping at the back of a boat as recorded in Mark 4:38-40.

> **Jesus was in the stern, sleeping on a cushion. The disciples woke him and said to him, "Teacher, don't you care if we drown?" He got up, rebuked the wind and said to the waves, "Quiet! Be still!" Then the wind died down and it was completely**

calm. He said to his disciples, "Why are you so afraid? Do you still have no faith?"

Mark 4:38-40, NIV

When Jesus calmed the wind and waves, he began to move his disciples from fear to faith.

Just like Jesus, you have the ability to influence and inspire others. No, it's not always easy, and you're sure to encounter a few storms along the way. Just remember that storms are an important part of the process. They build courage and make us stronger. They prepare us to be the captain of our own ship, to be the best possible leader for God and others.

What is a Leader?

In this book, we will spend a lot of time discussing Servant LeaderShip Wisdom. You will notice that I've capitalized the "S" in the word "LeaderShip." That's not a mistake. I want to emphasize the symbolism of water and boats, which are mentioned frequently in the Bible. I have spent nearly 50 years boating on the Great Lakes and the ocean, and I have experienced character-building events including severe storms, dense fog and significant emergency situations. To me, the word "Ship" is a reminder that we all must have faith in our ability to steer our own ships in the sea of life. We are all servants seeking God's wisdom.

God calls each one of us to seek the light continually, knowing we can't get there during our time on Earth. It's an ongoing process.

Find a Hurt and Heal It

There's a traditional marketing saying that instructs people to find a need and fill it. If we could sit and have a face-to-face conversation with Jesus today, chances are He wouldn't stop there. Robert H. Schuller of Crystal Cathedral in Garden Grove, California, once said at a leadership conference I attended that Jesus would probably challenge us to find a hurt and heal it.

It's a bigger, broader challenge, of course, but imagine what could happen if we all addressed the matters of the heart with love and service, 24/7.

> **And I tell you that you are Peter, and on this rock I will build my church, and the gates of Hades will not overcome it.**
>
> **Matthew 16:18, NIV**

This book is designed to help you become a better servant leader. Throughout each chapter, you will find several sets of thought-provoking questions. I encourage you to work through these questions independently or in a small group setting. Wrestle with the questions, and challenge yourself to live differently. You will also find blank journal pages at the end of this book. I invite you to jot down notes and ideas as you discover and grow.

Now, let's Discover Your **Next Best Step!** Let the journey begin!

Love, Serve and Pursue

Principle 1: Love God, Love and Serve Others, Pursue Your Passions

The Greatest Commandment

Love the Lord your God with all your heart and with all your soul and with all your strength.

Deuteronomy 6:5 NIV

Jesus replied: "'Love the Lord your God with all your heart and with all your soul and with all your mind.' This is the first and greatest commandment. And the second is like it: 'Love your neighbor as yourself.' All the Law and the Prophets hang on these two commandments."

Matthew 22:37-40, NIV

In the mid-1980s, I met Josiah Beecham, a Scottish pastor who delivered his final sermon while serving in New Buffalo, Michigan. It also happened to be a repeat of the first sermon he ever gave. His Message, "Love God and Serve Others," had a great impact on me. Somehow, that sermon simplified some of the complexity of the New Testament, illustrating how a servant leader should have a compassionate love of God, people and life. God intends for us to pursue our God-given passions. To me, this is at the heart and foundation of being a Servant Leader. It is scriptural, and everything ties to the two greatest commandments referenced above.

Seeking Beauty

Making hospital visits is one of my personal passions. Early on, a pastor who mentored me taught me to pause for a moment before entering a hospital room. "Every person you meet is the most beautiful person in the world," he said. "The beauty may not be evident right away, but it's there."

Upon reflection, I learned that he was not referring to external beauty. Instead, he was reminding me that in every person, there is a piece of Christ buried within.

> **I can do all this through him who gives me strength.**
>
> **Philippians 4:13, NIV**

It can be difficult to be confronted with the harsh realities of a serious illness. When making hospital visits, I strive to be present in the moment. When I spend time with someone who really doesn't know what his or her **Next Best Step** could possibly be, I just get this overwhelming feeling that I'm exactly where I'm supposed to be. Quite often the time spent sitting and praying with someone is immensely powerful, and I cherish the opportunity to feel God's presence in these quiet moments.

Be still, and know that I am God.

Psalm 46:10

Life Lesson/Points to Ponder

- How do you seek beauty in others?
- Can you share a time when you were intentionally quiet in an attempt to draw closer to God?
- What is your **Next Best Step**?

Never Give Up

I walked into the hospital room, and right away, I could tell that emotions were running high.

A young woman was in bed, and she was fighting for her life. Doctors said her chances of overcoming her extremely serious heart issues were slim, but I could sense her resolve.

The woman's husband, who sat in a nearby chair, looked spent. He'd been on an emotional rollercoaster, and it was apparent that the ups and downs of this ordeal were taking their toll.

The couple's children, meanwhile, were running around. It seemed they had no grasp on the seriousness of the situation, and they laughed and played as children do.

I walked over to the woman's bedside, introduced myself and remained quiet for a few moments. She began to tell me what was going on in her life, and I listened. After a short while I took her hand and began to pray. I asked for God's will to be done, which included asking for total healing. If that wasn't possible, I asked for direction regarding her **Next Best Step**. I began to feel an intense wave of energy flow from the woman's hand to mine, and I sensed that she was not going to give up. I've experienced this warmth and energy before, yet it's always moving.

Months later I happened to be doing hospital visits, and I learned that this same woman was very ill once again. As I worked my way to her room, I heard that she likely had only hours to live.

I entered her room and quietly took her hand. Despite the fact that she was unable to communicate, I could feel the same intense wave of energy as I prayed with her.

Doctors and nurses were coming and going, doing everything they could to save this woman. In time, to everyone's surprise, she pulled through once again.

The list of issues with this woman's health was long, and there never seemed to be much hope that she'd fully recover, yet she rebounded on four separate occasions during a period of several years.

About a year later I was at church. I noticed a woman looking my way, but I couldn't place her. As I walked toward the woman, I could see that she was wearing a wig. I took one look in her eyes and knew I was standing in front of the woman from the hospital. I told her what an inspiration she was to me, and she said, "Thank you for not giving up on me."

In December 2014, this woman received a new heart. She is not out of the woods, but she has an insatiable desire to live.

I had a chance to have lunch with her recently, and she told me that when doctors told her there was no hope, she refused to agree with them. She is still a fighter.

> **"Have I not commanded you? Be strong and courageous. Do not be afraid; do not be discouraged, for the Lord your God will be with you wherever you go."**
>
> **Joshua 1:9, NIV**

The woman also told me that she derived a lot of her strength from her grandfather, who survived the sinking of a ship in World War II. He spent three days in the ocean, not knowing whether he'd live or die. He was not a believer, but he said to God, "If I survive, I'll do whatever you want." Well, he made it -- and he eventually became a fire and brimstone pastor proclaiming God's love to one and all.

> **So do not fear, for I am with you; do not be dismayed, for I am your God. I will strengthen you and help you; I will uphold you with my righteous right hand.**
>
> **Isaiah 41:10, NIV**

We are commanded to love and care for others.

Life Lesson/Points to Ponder

- Sometimes you don't think you're making an impression or a difference. Have you ever found out months or years later that you've made a positive impact on someone's life?
- Are special connections or situations put before us by God to remind us that He knows we are following His plan for us or a reminder that the Holy Spirit is alive and well?
- How would the way you interact with people be different if you viewed each one as the most beautiful person in the world?
- What is your **Next Best Step**?

Returning Gracefully

Once, when making rounds at the hospital, a patient threw me out of his room.

"I don't know why you're here," he said angrily. "I've been an alcoholic my entire life. I did this to myself. I don't want any of that prayer stuff, and there's no reason for you to come back."

I turned to leave, but on my way out I noticed several piles of paperbacks on the man's nightstand.

The following week, I returned. I entered the room, and I could see that the man's daughter was visiting.

I said hello and then attempted to strike up a conversation. "I see you like to read." I picked up one of the books. "I've a read a few books by this author, too."

The man didn't say much, but he didn't ask me to leave, either.

We chatted for a few more minutes, and we prayed before I said goodbye.

As I looked back at my two encounters with this man, it occurred to me that my presence – welcome or not – still demonstrated God's love. I didn't give up, just as God doesn't give up on any of us.

Life Lesson/Points to Ponder

- Are there times when you gave up and wish you had given one more try or invested a little more in supporting someone?
- What would God say is the limit on the time you spend supporting others?
- How long does God support us?
- What is your **Next Best Step**?

Pursue Your Passions

Awhile back I was sharing the 10 Proven Principles of Servant LeaderShip Wisdom with a men's group at my church. At one point during the discussion, I had an idea. "Wouldn't it be neat if we had some kind of symbol to represent The Great Commission?"

It was a passing thought in the midst of that day's lesson, but after class one of the guys walked up to me and handed me a sketch. "What do you think of this?" he asked. I was blown away.

I played around with the sketch during the weekend and made some tweaks along the way. Then, I added the word "Go" in the center of the fish he had drawn.

A few days later, I was chatting with a friend who owns a marketing communications company. I told him about the sketch, and he offered to have his creative team come up with a few renderings.

In communicating with the artist, we discussed the symbolism behind the traditional Christian fish. In the first century, if a Christian were to approach someone as he walked through the woods, he would take his bow and lay it down. If the other person also happened to be a believer, he would lay down his bow in the opposite direction, forming the shape of a fish.

In designing this logo, I wanted to incorporate a thick, rugged image of a bow. But on the top, we decided to use a dashed line. The dashes represent my desire to look for people with whom I can share God's love. I am pursuing Christ, and I am pursuing others.

Months later, long after we'd crafted the "Go" logo, I saw a guy wearing a sweatshirt at the gym that said, "God's Power." I asked him about his sweatshirt, and before I knew it, I was showing him the logo.

He took a look and said, "You've got it wrong. The word in the middle shouldn't be "Go." It should be "Pursue."

Do you love God? Do you love others? How are you going to pursue your passions?

TM

Life Lesson/Points to Ponder

- What are some of the passions you would like to pursue further?
- How do you share God's love with others?
- What is your **Next Best Step**?

A quick recap of Principle 1: Love God, Love and Serve Others, Pursue Your Passions.

Vision and Journey

Principle 2: What Is Your Vision? Where Are You in the Journey? Listen Carefully

> **Where there is no vision, the people perish: but he that keepeth the law, happy is he.**
>
> **Proverbs 29:18 KJV**

> **Then I said to them, "You see the trouble we are in: Jerusalem lies in ruins, and its gates have been burned with fire. Come, let us rebuild the wall of Jerusalem, and we will no longer be in disgrace."**
>
> **Nehemiah 2:17, NIV**

Let Go and Let God

It's funny. We get in our cars these days, punch an address into a GPS device or a map app on our phones, and we're on our way. No need to be concerned about getting lost. The trusty automated voice – despite its often-funny inability to pronounce well-known street names – leads the way, instructing us to turn left at this stoplight or veer right at that fork in the road.

Wouldn't it be nice to have that kind of direction in all aspects of our lives?

Should I take the job?

What specifically can I do to strengthen my marriage?

How do I work my way through a period of profound grief?

Sometimes, life feels like a giant maze. It can be scary to make choices when we face an unexpected trial or come to a difficult crossroad. *Which way, Lord? Which way?*

We all have access to some exceptionally profound insight. We have the ability to worship an almighty God who can and will reveal His plan to us. God speaks to us through the Bible, through prayer and through other people. In our pursuit fully to understand God's will, it's up to us to ASK and LISTEN.

The answers will come, but know this – they don't always come as or when we expect, and we may not always like the answers we receive at the moment. Still, we have to be open to hear His answer and be patient. Rarely do things work as planned on the first go-round. Instead, we zig and zag in our quest to understand God's plan.

Life Lesson/Points to Ponder

- What is your Vision?
- Where are you in the journey as you strive to attain your Vision?
- What is your **Next Best Step**?

Nehemiah's Story

The walls of Jerusalem had fallen, and the entire town was in ruin. Nehemiah felt a tug on his heart to do something completely outrageous – he offered to rebuild the walls. He prayed to the God of Heaven, receiving affirmation from the Lord. With the King's support, Nehemiah left his job as a cupbearer and pursued his passion and purpose – to rebuild the walls of Jerusalem.

> **And because the gracious hand of my God was on me, the king granted my requests.**
> **Nehemiah 2:8b, NIV**

It doesn't matter where you are in life. It's important continually to ask these questions ... again and again and again. Ask the same questions of those you are leading, coaching or mentoring. It is definitely a process, and it's important to make sure your heart and mind are in alignment with God's will.

> **And let us run with perseverance the race marked out for us, fixing our eyes on Jesus,**

the pioneer and perfecter of faith. For the joy set before him he endured the cross, scorning its shame, and sat down at the right hand of the throne of God.

Hebrews 12:1b-2, NIV

Ask yourself the following questions:

What's my Vision?

Where am I in the Journey?

Am I listening carefully to God?

But don't stop there. As servant leaders, we must ask these questions of others, too. This is how we build teams and families.

What is YOUR Vision?

Where are you in YOUR Journey?

Are you listening carefully to God?

Ask these questions, then wait upon the Lord. Be still and listen carefully. The answers you hear will be pivotal as you determine your **Next Best Step.** The questions are universal, but the answers surely are not. What comes of this ongoing exploration will be unique to you. The outcome will be guided entirely by your vision and God's will.

I will instruct you and teach you in the way you should go; I will counsel you with my loving eye on you.

Psalm 32:8, NIV

A Secret to Success

Having a vision is imperative, no matter what your daily agenda may be. You can't get up every morning and just go through the motions – you have to have some idea of what you're working toward. This is a solid approach that applies to virtually every aspect of your life.

Mitch Kruse, a longtime friend and mentor, had a professor who once said, "If you know where you want to go, but you don't have a map, you're not going to end up there."

Of course, it's important to remember we're not traveling a straight path. Sometimes, when we ask these questions, we realize that we've taken a few steps backward. Other times, it becomes clear that we need to change our vision altogether. Keep asking, and keep moving in the direction God is leading you.

Life Lesson/Points to Ponder

- How can you tell when your vision has become more self-serving and less God-serving?
- How do you know if you are living according to God's will?

- Do you need to make any adjustments in your life?
- What is your **Next Best Step**?

Changing Course

> **I lift up my eyes to the mountains—where does my help come from? My help comes from the Lord, the Maker of heaven and earth. He will not let your foot slip—he who watches over you will not slumber; indeed, he who watches over Israel will neither slumber nor sleep. The Lord watches over you—the LORD is your shade at your right hand; the sun will not harm you by day, nor the moon by night. The LORD will keep you from all harm—he will watch over your life; the Lord will watch over your coming and going both now and forevermore.**
>
> **Psalm 121, NIV**

I was in an evening Bible Study Fellowship program with a group of guys, and one of them asked me if I could help him find a company to buy. He wanted to leave corporate America and run a business of his own.

"Sure," I said, and then I probed a little further. "What's your vision?"

He had a very clear vision of the life plan he wanted to achieve. He knew where he wanted to live, and he had an idea of how God would work within that vision.

> **Be strong and very courageous. Be careful to obey all the law my servant Moses gave you; do not turn from it to the right or the left, that you may be successful wherever you go. Keep this Book of the Law always on your lips; meditate on it day and night, so that you may be careful to do everything written in it. Then you will be prosperous and successful. Have I not commanded you? Be strong and courageous. Do not be afraid; do not be discouraged, for the Lord your God will be with you wherever you go.**
>
> **Joshua 1:7-9, NIV**

The man had also done some thinking about the types of businesses that aligned with his strengths and the strengths of his relatives. Ultimately, he was looking to begin a business venture that would include several family members.

Big changes, but sometimes that's what God leads us to do. He felt the call to make a change, and he was ready to take action.

Early in the process, I met frequently with the man and his wife.

"Life will be different," I told them. "You're used to being the vice president of a multi-billion-dollar company. Being the owner of a much smaller company won't be the same. You will be responsible for everything, including administrative tasks such as filing, banking, and managing human resources. There may be a day when you look at your wife and say, 'We can't make payroll this Friday. We're going to have to sacrifice a bit more.'"

They asked lots of questions, and together they listened, learned, and pursued God's will.

> **"For I know the plans I have for you," declares the Lord, "plans to prosper you and not to harm you, plans to give you hope and a future."**
>
> **Jeremiah 29:11, NIV**

I helped them develop a team of advisors – legal, accounting, and banking -- who could provide support throughout their journey, and they jumped right in.

God was faithful. In the span of 10 years, they acquired four companies that aligned with their original vision, and their journey continues today. Even through life's ups and downs they keep their focus in check, and they know their faith in God is at the root of it all.

> **Do not conform to the pattern of this world, but be transformed by the renewing of your mind. Then you will be able to test and approve what God's will is – his good, pleasing and perfect will.**
>
> **Romans 12:2, NIV**

Life Lesson/Points to Ponder

- What happens when you live your vision?
- What happens when you don't?
- Have you shared your vision with anybody?
- What is your **Next Best Step**?

Life's Detours: The Journey Unfolds

> **He replied, "Because you have so little faith. Truly I tell you, if you have faith as small as a mustard seed, you can say to this mountain, 'Move from here to there,' and it will move. Nothing will be impossible for you."**
>
> **Matthew 17:20, NIV**

In June of 1966, I was working at a restaurant called The Farmer's Daughter. I had just graduated from high school, and business at the restaurant was in full swing. I was out shopping one day with a friend, and the two of us ran into one of the waitresses at the restaurant. "Wait 'til you see the new waitress the manager hired!"

"When's she working?" I asked.

I learned the new waitress would be working that night, but I was scheduled to be off. It didn't matter. I figured I'd stop by anyway to check out this young woman whom I'd heard so much about.

Within a month, we had arranged a date. Pat and I went to a concert and dinner, and we talked for hours about our visions and dreams. We continued our conversation in her parents' driveway late into the night, realizing that we had an undeniable connection. Before I left, I asked Pat for a second date, suggesting that we get together on Sunday. "Meet me at 9 o'clock," she said. I was confused. Starting a date at 9 p.m. seemed kind of odd, but Pat had something else in mind. "Let's join my parents at church and we can go back to the house for lunch." I said yes.

Four months later, Pat and I were engaged on her birthday. Together, we identified three goals:

1. I wanted to develop a meaningful relationship with Christ.
2. I wanted to become a United States citizen.
3. We both wanted to establish financial security as we began our lives together.

While we dated, I opened my heart to God's love. In 1968, I made a profession of faith before the consistory of the Hope Reformed Church in Chicago. We'd accomplished our first goal.

On August 16, 1969, Pat and I were married. A few months later, as we prepared to celebrate our first Thanksgiving as a married couple, I became a citizen of the United States of America in Hammond, Indiana, on Nov. 24, 1969. I was born in Canada, and although my family had moved to the United States when I was three years old, I always wondered if my parents would move back. Becoming a citizen was a very proud moment for me. We'd accomplished our second goal.

During our courtship and the early years of our marriage, I worked at a restaurant, a steel mill, a construction company, and a sod farm. Working multiple jobs was grueling, but the money I earned allowed me to pay for my college education and establish financial security. We had accomplished our third goal.

> **Never be lacking in zeal, but keep your spiritual fervor, serving the Lord. Be joyful in hope, patient in affliction, faithful in prayer.**
>
> **Romans 12:11-12, NIV**

Pat and I had always talked about having children, and we were ready to start our family. Like some couples, we discovered we were facing infertility problems. Our dream of having a big family felt very much out of reach.

Still, we never lost faith. We prayed about our desire to have children. We saw countless doctors, and we began the journey to pursue adoption. We knew there were families who were not able to rear the children they had conceived, but we kept running into roadblocks.

Well-meaning family and friends would often inquire about our future plans. "Aren't you planning to have children?" they would ask. Social pressures made this time of our lives challenging.

And then, things changed in the blink of an eye. We were visiting relatives in Chicago in 1974, and Pat's cousin Harry –

a lawyer – asked us how things were going. For some reason, we decided to open up about our struggles. He said, "I wish I had known all of this. I just helped place a child into a home."

The next day, Harry called Pat to tell her about a baby who would be available for adoption in July. Our lives changed in an instant. We loved James Christopher before he was born, and we accepted financial responsibility for rearing a child long before we knew what would happen. Welcoming Jim into our family was a certain answer to prayer.

Two years later we learned from a consistory member about another young woman looking for an adoptive family for her unborn baby. We jumped at the chance to expand our family once again. We know that our son Matthew Alexander was another answer to prayer.

For many years, we remained a happy family of four. Then, as our boys reached adulthood, our family began to multiply once again.

Jim was married, and in 1998, he and his wife welcomed our first granddaughter, Victoria Michele. Two years later, Jim's family was blessed again with the arrival of twin girls, Alexandria Ann and Alivia Joy.

In August 2007, our son Matt married his wife Jamie, and in 2012, we were thrilled to welcome our first grandson, Dublin James.

But, life doesn't always go according to plan. In 2013, Jim and his wife divorced.

To our surprise, that wasn't the end of the story. Jim remarried in 2015, and we welcomed Jennifer and her four children -- Eleanor Grace, Lauren Olivia, Kathryn Nicole and Maya Jane -- into the family. That same year, Matt and Jamie welcomed a beautiful daughter, Aria Leigh. Today, we are blessed beyond measure with two sons, two daughters-in-law and nine grandchildren and step-grandchildren. How amazing! Through the miracle of adoption, grandchildren and a blended family, we ended up having the huge family we first talked about 50 years earlier.

> **And now these three remain: faith, hope and love. But the greatest of these is love.**
> **1 Corinthians 13:13, NIV**

Today, our goal is to pass on faith, hope and love to each and every member of our family.

Life Lesson/Points to Ponder

- Are there roadblocks in your life that you struggled with in your family or extended family?
- Were you trusting of God as you took steps forward toward a solution?
- Were you quick to give God the glory when you moved beyond the challenge?
- What is your **Next Best Step**?

An Unexpected Change of Plans

As a businessperson, my goal is to help companies build and grow, and acquisitions are one way to work toward that end result.

One day, I met with the president of one of the best-run family companies in Chicago. The family wanted to diversify the company's business risks, and we discussed the possibility of acquiring a new business platform in a different industry that demonstrated upside growth and above-average profitability. We both felt that this was the **Next Best Step** for his company.

Once I understood this family's personal, financial and business goals, I knew which of my longtime business contacts I should pursue. I was on a mission to find a company that might be a good fit for the team in Chicago, and I figured someone would be able to help me find the right match. Interestingly, several of my contacts told me to call Dave, the owner of a company in northern Indiana.

I called Dave, and we agreed to meet at a Bob Evans restaurant. Dave's son-in-law Wade was with him, and the three of us proceeded to chat. My intent was to keep things casual, allowing ample time to get to know one another before discussing business. Mostly, I wanted Dave and Wade to feel comfortable as they shared a little bit about their history, vision, and journey.

The more we talked, I could see that Dave's heart was completely open to God's calling. He was willing to consider selling his company to the folks in Chicago, and he immediately announced his plans to his employees. In my experience, most business owners don't do this so early in the process.

Dave says he often turned to this verse:

> **Trust in the Lord with all your heart and lean not on your own understanding; in all your ways submit to him, and he will make your paths straight.**
>
> **Proverbs 3: 5-6, NIV**

Dave's decision to announce the sale of the company may have seemed rash, but I can tell you that it was not. Dave cared greatly for his employees, and he had no intention of letting a new owner put them in a bad position. He never lost sight of the fact he wanted the best for his team with God leading the way.

His confidence was completely uncharacteristic of others in his shoes. During the next few weeks and months, he never flinched. He opened his heart, doors, and books to the prospective investor.

When a deal like this is on the table, things can change at a moment's notice. I had gotten to know the folks at this company, and they had nothing but my utmost admiration and respect. If the deal somehow fell through, I had no intention of walking away. It was clear that the company had the potential to become incredibly successful. This was largely because of Dave's daily display of servant leadership and his unshakeable faith in God. He always put himself last, demonstrated extreme humility, and lived a very simple, God-focused life.

In the 11th hour and the 59th minute, the Chicago investor decided not to proceed. Now what? Dave was undaunted.

It didn't take long for us to realize that a better plan was in store. Dave's son-in-law Wade and his wife Lisa had been trying to figure out their own journey in the midst of the Chicago negotiations. When the Chicago plan fell through, Wade was faced with an unexpected opportunity to acquire his father-in-law's company. We shifted gears immediately.

> **No temptation has overtaken you except what is common to mankind. And God is faithful; he will not let you be tempted beyond what you can bear. But when you are tempted, he will also provide a way out so that you can endure it.**
>
> **1 Corinthians 10:13, NIV**

Dave's vision remained the same: to ensure the continued success of his company and make sure his longtime employees were in good hands. And Wade's vision, which had never really been a part of the main conversation, was once again in clear focus.
The journey changed, and we marched on.

Within four years, the company had more than doubled in size. Even more important: the company's God-focused culture remains intact.

What's my Vision?

Where am I in the Journey?

Am I listening carefully to God?

These questions – and answers – are a huge part of any journey. Be sure to come back to them again and again.

> **Plans fail for lack of counsel, but with many advisers they succeed.**
>
> **Proverbs 15:22, NIV**

Life Lesson/Points to Ponder

- How can you know steadfastly that you're living a "God plan" and not a "me plan?"
- When do you share your experiences with others?
- When or how long do you listen with your heart?
- What is your **Next Best Step**?

A quick recap of Principle 2: What Is Your Vision? Where Are You in the Journey? Listen Carefully.

Culture

Principle 3: Develop a Culture with People Who Are Humble, Wise, Want to Do Their Best and Have Fun

> **Walk with the wise and become wise, for a companion of fools suffers harm.**
>
> **Proverbs 13:20, NIV**

The Best People

When I was in my 30s, I read a reprint of a letter that the founder of the Marriott hotel chain had given to his son as he handed over leadership of the company to him. The letter, as you might guess, was chock-full of wonderful thoughts and ideas about running a company and taking proper care of oneself along the way. It was filled with golden nuggets of information, but one credo really stood out to me: Surround yourself with great people who want to win and have fun.

I'm here to tell you, that little gem is a game changer in all aspects of your life.

In fact, it's really not new advice. If you've ever found yourself running with the wrong crowd, there's a good chance at least one well-meaning adult reminded you that you're known by the company you keep. So true.

No matter where we are in life, it's critical for us to surround ourselves with like-minded people who challenge us to be the best we can be. This is fundamental to success.

> **Therefore encourage one another and build each other up, just as in fact you are doing.**
> **1 Thessalonians 5:11, NIV**

Jesus chose to surround himself with 12 disciples. They were an eclectic group, but they each supported Him in different ways.

> **Jesus went up on a mountainside and called to him those he wanted, and they came to him.**
> **Mark 3:13, NIV**

However, just as a supportive group will build you up, a non-supportive group of friends will have the opposite effect. My dad used to tell me that life is a series of choices. If I ever found myself in bad situation, he said, just run. A few years later, when I was working as a teacher's assistant at Purdue University, a bunch of students invited me to hang out with them. It wasn't long before they were up to no good, and I immediately remembered my dad's words. *Just run.*

Do not be misled: "Bad company corrupts good character."

1 Corinthians 15:33, NIV

Do the people who you spend the most time with day after day build you up or tear you down? If they're not nudging you in the right direction, it may be time to choose a different circle. You will rise or fall based on the company you keep.

Life Lesson/Points to Ponder

- Do you have someone you admire and see as a role model?
- Have you considered scheduling a regular time to seek out or meet with this person one-on-one?
- How can you best develop a mentor relationship?
- What is your **Next Best Step**?

An Unlikely Camaraderie

When I began my first job, I was 24 and pretty green. I started at the bottom, doing new product development in a one-person department.

I listened and learned, quickly working my way through the ranks. As I took on greater levels of responsibility, I would hear employees say things like, "I've got kids older than you." I never let it bother me. I just kept on doing my job and learning from those around me.

In the span of a little more than a decade I had worked my way to the top, moving into the role of chairman and president of the company. I always believed I could succeed, but my success wouldn't have been possible without the support of others who believed in me, too.

I had numerous mentors along the way. My first business mentor, the founder of a manufacturing company, suggested I take a Dale Carnegie speech class. I honed my ability to speak in public, developed confidence, and learned valuable techniques to manage worry. Dean was an electric public speaker, and he taught me how to be creative and take calculated risks in product development and sales. He encouraged a creative, outside-the-box approach to solving problems.

My next business mentor, Sandy, emphasized the importance of relationships. He taught me how to run a business with love and respect, all the while keeping safety and housekeeping a top priority. He was a stickler for consistent quality and on-time delivery while making a profit. These skills have been instrumental throughout my life, both at work and at home.

> **God gave Solomon wisdom and very great insight, and a breadth of understanding as measureless as the sand on the seashore.**
>
> **1 Kings 4:29, NIV**

As I settled into my new role as company president, I once again found myself working amidst a diverse and talented group of leaders. Everyone in the group had worked at Alcoa, a world-class company, and everyone was 20 to 30 years older than I was.

We were a team in every sense of the word. We met every week, reviewed our results every month, and developed our strategy and budget annually. We enjoyed some good times together, and, on occasion, we played golf and tennis or shared a meal together with our wives. We worked together for 17 years, each bringing different skills to the table. Eventually, we even had the chance to become owners of the company together. As I look back, it's inspiring to see how we grew together.

> **When they had finished eating, Jesus said to Simon Peter, "Simon son of John, do you love me more than these?" "Yes, Lord," he said, "you know that I love you." Jesus said, "Feed my lambs."**
>
> **John 21:15, NIV**

You have to understand people's needs, wants, and hurts in order to feed Jesus' lambs. We were a cohesive team, and as we grew together, we tried to be good examples of God's love by caring for the people, our lambs, in our work community.

Of course, we had plenty of ups and downs along the way, but we relied on each other in good and bad times. Throughout the years we suffered the loss of a company founder, dealt with the costly effects of inflation, and figured out how to rebound from some significant losses in business. Time and again we worked together, and you know what? We always managed to find our way to the other side.

Life Lesson/Points to Ponder

- What defines success to you?
- Do you have a way to measure if you're on a Christ-like path?
- What is your **Next Best Step**?

A Gentle Nudge

I have a longtime client who is extremely fortunate to have a dynamic leadership team.

I've worked with this client's company on numerous projects, including acquisitions, strategic planning, and business development seminars. I even helped mentor one young executive, watching him in his journey from vice president of sales to chairman of the company.

The entire leadership team at this particular company is made up of believers, and they've developed a healthy culture and an unwavering sense of cohesiveness.

Sometimes, though, they need a little nudge – and that's when they call me. They know I'll push them. I'll challenge them to move projects and companywide initiatives to the **Next Best Step**. "Push forward," I tell them, and I show them how to take a bold step forward with the appropriate risk.

When you know there's a tough task on the table, assemble the right team. With God's wisdom, you'll know exactly who you need on your side.

Life Lesson/Points to Ponder

- Do you surround yourself with the best people?
- What could you change about yourself? What can you do better?
- What is your **Next Best Step**?

A quick recap of Principle 3: Develop a Culture with People Who Are Humble, Wise, Want to Do Their Best and Have Fun.

Trust

Principle 4: Nurture a Caring Attitude, Create a Sense of Trust

> **You will keep in perfect peace those whose minds are steadfast, because they trust in you. Trust in the Lord forever, for the Lord, the Lord himself, is the Rock eternal.**
>
> **Isaiah 26:3-4, NIV**

> **Whatever happens, conduct yourselves in a manner worthy of the gospel of Christ. Then, whether I come and see you or only hear about you in my absence, I will know that you stand firm in the one Spirit, striving together as one for the faith and the gospel.**
>
> **Philippians 1:27, NIV**

A Baby Steals Their Hearts

In 1979, I had an opportunity to attend the Alcoa Management Conference in Pittsburgh. I was working for Alcoa at its Lincoln subsidiary, and this conference was the company's way of developing executives for internal leadership promotions.

One afternoon those attending the conference settled in for a presentation on safety. Boy, were we surprised when a guy by the name of Big Jim walked to the front of the room with a baby in his arms.

You could hear murmurs and whispers throughout the room, as no one knew quite what to make of the baby in the arms of this burly man. Big Jim had been one of the best managers at one of the company's biggest facilities. He lived and breathed safety, and we couldn't figure out how a baby related to the topic at hand.

We soon learned that the baby was Big Jim's grandchild. As he walked back and forth in front of us, he talked about all the work and effort that goes into rearing a child. You have to feed a child and make sure he or she is getting proper nutrition. You need to bathe the child and change dirty diapers. You need to dress the child in clean clothes, and when the baby becomes mobile, you need keep him or her out of harm's way.

Big Jim then explained that on-the-job safety requires the same level of around-the-clock attentiveness. Everyone was responsible for enforcing the company's core principles – safety and housekeeping. On the factory floor, it was our job to keep our eyes open. Christ also expects us to take care of one another.

> **"A new command I give you: Love one another. As I have loved you, so you must love one another. By this everyone will know that you are my disciples, if you love one another."**
>
> **John 13:34-35, NIV**

Life Lesson/Points to Ponder

- When have you displayed unwavering care for others?
- How can you show a caring attitude on a daily basis?
- What is your **Next Best Step**?

Listen to Their Hearts

In 1989, about 10 years after hearing Big Jim's presentation on safety, I found myself in the process of changing jobs. I was going to be the CEO of a very large holding company that had factories throughout the Midwest, on the East Coast, and in parts of the South.

About a week before I started the new job, the owner called me and said an employee had been killed in one of the factories. The owner was concerned about this tragedy, and he asked me what I would do to manage such a situation.

We talked about his **Next Best Step**, and I suggested that he go visit the factory and reach out to his employees. He needed to demonstrate his concern because everyone was undoubtedly struggling with this situation.

A few weeks later, I started my new role as CEO. The next day, I started making rounds at all of the factories to meet all of the 1100 employees. We met in small groups, and it was not uncommon for me to tell people that a lot of what I learned and practiced came directly from the Bible. I tried to practice the Golden Rule.

> **Trust in the Lord with all your heart and lean not on your own understanding; in all your ways submit to him, and he will make your paths straight.**
>
> **Proverbs 3:5-6, NIV**

> **Do to others as you would have them do to you.**
>
> **Luke 6:31, NIV**

When I arrived at the facility where the employee had been killed, I continued meeting with employees in small groups – but I did something else, too. I told everyone I would return the following week to meet every employee individually.

I arrived at midnight and met each of the folks working third shift. When the first-shift crew began to arrive, I continued introducing myself to everyone. It was a long day, but I stayed until I'd met those working second shift, as well.

I asked each employee to tell me what improvements needed to be made, and I just listened. I didn't take notes or jot down names. I simply wanted to hear what each person had to say.

It didn't take long to figure out what needed to change, and in short order, we began to turn things around.

I started by doing a presentation similar to the one I'd heard Big Jim give. Interesting how God had prepared me 10 years earlier for this tough challenge. There was a secretary at the company who had a young baby, and I filled her in on the plan. She allowed me to introduce her child to the workforce, and I shared with everyone my hope that we would be just as attentive with one another as we were with young children. Yes, we needed to focus on quality, service, and cost, but in order to be successful, we needed to start with the basics. We needed to demonstrate our love and care for our fellow man, just as we do with our children. Everyone took the message to heart, and before long the culture throughout the factory changed dramatically.

> **In the same way, let your light shine before others, that they may see your good deeds and glorify your Father in heaven.**
>
> **Matthew 5:16, NIV**

As servant leaders, walking the walk is more important than talking the talk.

Life Lesson/Points to Ponder

- Have you ever humbled yourself for the greater good of a tough situation? Give examples.
- Does your leadership reflect the care and compassion you would offer a child or a member of your family?
- What is your **Next Best Step**?

A quick recap of Principle 4: Nurture a Caring Attitude, Create a Sense of Trust.

Excellence

Principle 5: Strive for Excellence in All You Do

> **Finally, brothers and sisters, whatever is true, whatever is noble, whatever is right, whatever is pure, whatever is lovely, whatever is admirable – if anything is excellent or praiseworthy – think about such things. Whatever you have learned or received or heard from me, or seen in me – put it into practice. And the God of peace will be with you.**
>
> **Philippians 4:8-9, NIV**

A Humble Servant Leader

Every so often you meet or work with somebody who makes a profound impact on your life. I'm talking about the kind of person who changes you deep down inside, someone who shapes the very core of your being.

Your initial interactions may not seem terribly profound, but as you look in life's rearview mirror years later, you realize just how much of an impact that person made.

Sandy was just that kind of person. He was my boss for 15 years, but he was also my mentor. He groomed me from the time I was a young vice president, preparing me and shaping me for the role of president and then chairman. His wisdom and guidance helped me become a seasoned leader.

When it came to running a company, Sandy believed in the importance of safety, quality, and service. No matter what, everyone needed to demonstrate unwavering care for the customer, the employee, and the supplier. Our goal – on the good days and the bad -- was to continue our march toward excellence.

Sandy was a man of few words. His preferred leadership style was to listen and ponder. Sometimes, I'd go to him with what I thought was a great idea, and he'd say, "Thank you. We can talk about it later." I thought, "Why wait?" but I respected Sandy's patient and thoughtful business approach as time went on.

When I took over as chairman and president, I moved into Sandy's office. His modest desk was completely empty except for a single article, *The Human Side of Enterprise* by Douglas McGregor. Sandy was handing over the reins of an entire company, and all he chose to leave behind was that article. To me, it symbolized his faith in me. It was as if he was saying, *Remember this, and you'll do just fine.*

At one point in my career, Sandy demonstrated his faith in my leadership abilities by recommending I attend the Alcoa

Management Conference. I thought I was going to compete against the other 35 attendees for a chance to be promoted within the company. I couldn't have been more wrong. The invitation-only conference was a prime opportunity to develop my leadership skills further in the company with some of the other emerging leaders. We were all a team, and we learned from one another.

As my perspective changed, I began to really understand the value of being part of a team. We shared a common mission, and together we were stronger as a unit than any one of us could have been singly. Perspective helps us all recognize and appreciate each other's strengths and differences.

Continuous Improvement

Excellence is a moving target.

In pursuing excellence, you will always find a better way to address challenges or a way to cut costs. This is called Continuous Improvement. To me, it applies to life – not just business.

Part of being a good manager is being a good steward of all that has been entrusted to you. Remember this: People, time and money are your most valuable resources, and it's important to treat these resources with great care.

> **Not that I have already obtained all this, or have already arrived at my goal, but I press**

on to take hold of that for which Christ Jesus took hold of me.

Philippians 3:12, NIV

Of course, the desire to achieve excellence has far-reaching implications in all areas of your life. You can strive to be a better mom or to create a healthier lifestyle, always with a focus on Christ and eternal life. The point is to do your best – always.

Additionally, when you realize that something is amiss, act quickly. If you discover a failing process at work, fix it. If you're struggling in your marriage, fix it. If your relationship with Christ is falling short, fix it.

Whatever you do, work at it with all your heart, as working for the Lord, not for human masters.

Colossians 3:23, NIV

Life Lesson/Points to Ponder

- Who in your life has had a profound influence and why? How can you learn from them to promote excellence within yourself?
- In what areas of your life do you need to change your strategy to move excellence forward?
- What is your **Next Best Step**?

An Impeccable Business Model

A close friend of mine was among the most successful Pizza Hut franchisees in the world. Dick was one of my customers.

I remember asking Dick what it was about his operating style that allowed his business to be No. 1 for more than three decades. Instead of just answering the question, he invited me to go on a ride with him.

We drove around town for a few hours, visiting a handful of his successful Pizza Hut restaurants. As we approached each one, I could see right away that everything was always in its place. The roof was not your typical cherry red. Instead, it was a rich, natural wood. The signs were attractive and uniform. Inside, I immediately felt at ease, thanks to an attractive, homey atmosphere. The booths, the drapes, the table décor … it all made me feel like I was enjoying the comfort of a friend's invitation into his home. Dick wanted the best for each of his customers.

> **Therefore, as we have opportunity, let us do good to all people, especially to those who belong to the family of believers."**
>
> **Galatians 6:10, NIV**

Upon entering one of the restaurants, one of Dick's managers asked if he could run a special promotion. Dick's reply: "Sure, as long as you have your house in order."

"What do you mean by that?" I asked.

Dick explained. "When you have guests over to your home, what do you do? You vacuum, you dust, and you make sure everything is just as it should be. Same thing here. I want my managers and employees to treat these restaurants with the same kind of care. It puts guests at ease. It makes them feel as if they are right at home."

This is true in all areas of life. Taking the time to tend to small details often reaps large rewards.

> **Not looking to your own interests but each of you to the interests of others.**
>
> **Philippians 2:4, NIV**

I probed further. "What is it about your food, your prices, and your people that is different?"

Dick expounded a little more about his philosophy. "I share a percentage of my current profits with the management, I provide better value to my customers, I use only the best ingredients, and my prices are competitive." In fact, Dick even included his father – a former tent preacher – in the role of quality control manager. What better person than a preacher to be in charge of quality control?

Just as I had learned in the past, it's important to care for the customer, the employee, and the supplier.

Life Lesson/Points to Ponder

- What are some key takeaways from Dick's approach? What can we learn from his business philosophy?

- In what ways can you improve how you treat others?
- What is your **Next Best Step**?

Cutting Corners Comes at a Cost

When I became president of a large manufacturing company, a man by the name of Chick succeeded me as vice president. He was responsible for our company's product line from a marketing perspective.

Chick came into my office one day, and he could barely contain himself. He said he had identified a huge cost-reduction strategy, and he suggested we implement it immediately.

We were in the business of manufacturing a very high-quality, professional-grade aluminum cooking utensil for the foodservice industry, and like any other manufacturer, cost reduction was always top of mind.

Chick handed me an 8-ounce aluminum measuring cup, saying it was a suitable and cost-effective replacement for an existing product that had been part of our line for many years. It would cost less to make, Chick said, and it would perform the same function as the old.

I wasn't impressed. I reached out and crushed it with one hand.

Chick was stunned.

Quality and excellence were our business, I explained. We have a reputation for picking the best aluminum alloy, developing the best tooling and creating long-lasting products that withstand the test of time. All those benefits came at a cost. We didn't want to cut corners and compromise our good name.

Years later, while I was working for a different company, Chick showed up at my office. He told me I'd been more than a boss – I'd been a teacher. Then he handed me a gift-wrapped box.

Inside, I found that crushed measuring cup, a symbol of the lesson I'd taught Chick. Strive for excellence in all you do.

> **If anyone builds on this foundation using gold, silver, costly stones, wood, hay or straw, their work will be shown for what it is, because the Day will bring it to light. It will be revealed with fire, and the fire will test the quality of each person's work.**
>
> **1 Corinthians 3:12-13, NIV**

Life Lesson/Points to Ponder

- What are some repercussions of compromise and cutting corners?

- What are the reasons we would always teach by example?

- What is your **Next Best Step**?

A quick recap of Principle 5: Strive for Excellence in All You Do.

Commitment

Principle 6: Serve Others and Keep Your Commitments

> **Commit to the Lord whatever you do, and**
> **he will establish your plans.**
> **Proverbs 16:3, NIV**

The Value in Keeping Your Word

As a company executive, I had an open-door policy. Anybody could drop in if they wanted to discuss something with me. One day, a man by the name of Harley walked into my office.

"Do you think all of our products should be delivered on time?" he asked.

"Of course," I responded. Harley has a way of eventually making his point.

"Do you think we should have any broken promises?" he probed a little further.

"No, that would be terrible," I said.

Harley went on to explain that he was in charge of scheduling at the factory, and it wasn't uncommon for orders to be late or incomplete for any number of reasons. With so many people involved in day-to-day operations, there was always room for something to go wrong.

"I have an idea," he finally said. "Why don't you send a note to the troops telling them that all shipments will be on time and that we will have no broken promises?"

Seemed logical, but I wanted to know why Harley couldn't be the person to relay that message to his team. Harley and I had known each other for more than 10 years, and he always had really good ideas. He told me he wanted help because he cared about our customers, he cared about our employees, and he wanted to find a way to improve the entire process.

A day or so later I sent out a note saying that I expected all orders to be filled on time. Furthermore, if there was some sort of holdup that prevented us from completing an order, I needed to know about it. Bottom line: If we, as a company, were about to break a promise, then we needed to communicate that to our customers. We needed to get everything out in the open.

For the next several weeks, a pattern emerged. I'd get to work about 7:15 a.m., and sure enough, there'd be a pile of notes on my desk. "The metal didn't come in, so we couldn't get this particular shipment out," or "We had a production machine go down before a run was complete."

Within a few weeks, however, the notes began to decrease.

Little by little, employees were beginning to take ownership of the work they were doing, and demonstrating pride. They didn't want to represent the broken link in an otherwise sturdy chain.

As servant leaders, we *care*. It becomes our mission to do a job well. With time, we realize that it's no fun to break promises or let others down – and if something *is* going to interfere with our plan, we should get it out in the open and make things right.

> **The Lord detests lying lips, but he delights in people who are trustworthy.**
> **Proverbs 12:22, NIV**

The emphasis here is on keeping your commitments. If you plan to serve others, you have to keep your promises. When you do this, you gain trust, and that pleases our God. He delights in people who are trustworthy.

As a leader, it's important to hold people accountable. People do what you *inspect*, not what you *expect* – and, ultimately, Christ inspects what we do. We are accountable to Him. He is inspecting all the time.

Here's another verse that makes the same point a little differently:

Let your word be 'Yes, Yes," or 'No, No'; anything more than this comes from the evil one.

Matthew 5:37, NRSV

This wonderful verse emphasizes the importance of building the kind of relationships in which people can count on one another *always*. You know the kind of person I'm talking about: someone who says he or she is going to do something and you know you never have to think about it again. It's done.

Life Lesson/Points to Ponder

- It's not good to break a promise, but if you absolutely have to, how best should you go about it? Give an example.

- In what ways did Jesus give us the example of being a servant?

- How do you show that you are trustworthy to God? (We put our trust in God, but can he put His trust in us?)

- What is your **Next Best Step**?

When In Doubt, Pray

Sometimes, we all get a little stuck.

Back in the late 80s, we were looking for a new foreman to take over for a gentleman who had served us for decades. This particular area of the factory was responsible for finishing our products and making them as good as they could be. It was a very demanding area of work, and it required a lot of skill and attention to detail.

A longtime and hardworking employee named Roger was being considered for the position, but he was reluctant to accept the promotion. The job was his if he wanted it, but he just wasn't sure.

One day, while walking the factory floor, I saw Roger.

"I understand that you've been offered the foreman slot. Do you understand what it takes to make the product?" I asked.

"Oh, yes, Gord. I sure do."

"Do you know how to operate this work center in a safe way while maintaining good housekeeping?"

"Of course," he said.

"Do you know all the people in this work center?"

"You know I do," he said. "I've been here for years."

"Do you love them?" I asked. "In other words, do you care for them?"

He looked at me and said that he did.

I asked one last question. "Do you believe in the power of prayer?"

When he said yes, I urged him to go home and pray about his decision during the weekend. We all knew he was the right person for the job.

Roger came in Monday, and to my delight, he accepted the position. Although he had been on the fence, he decided to make a commitment to serving the company and the employees. He cared for them. And you know what? Just as I expected, he did an excellent job.

> **So then, brothers and sisters, stand firm and hold fast to the teachings we passed on to you, whether by word of mouth or by letter.**
> **2 Thessalonians 2:15, NIV**

Life Lesson/Points to Ponder

- Sometimes we don't have confidence in ourselves. How does a servant leader influence the decision of a person who is on the fence about change in their life?
- How much emphasis do you place on prayer?
- How do you show people that you value them so they are empowered to make decisions and take chances?
- What is your **Next Best Step**?

A quick recap of Principle 6: Serve Others and Keep Your Commitments.

Stewardship

Principle 7: Be a Thoughtful Steward of God's Capital and Focus Carefully on Results

> **The man who had received five bags of gold brought the other five. 'Master,' he said, 'you entrusted me with five bags of gold. See, I have gained five more.' His master replied, 'Well done, good and faithful servant! You have been faithful with a few things; I will put you in charge of many things. Come and share your master's happiness!'**
>
> **Matthew 25:20-21, NIV**

An Unexpected Messenger

In the late 1980s, I became the president of a holding company. With seven locations and more than 1,000 people making building products for the residential market, it was a large-scale operation – but times were tough. America was in the midst of a recession, and housing starts were at an all-time low. Demand for our product was soft, and job cuts were imminent. Some employees would likely lose their jobs entirely; others would see a significant reduction in hours.

I happened to be walking the aisles of our plastics factory in Olive Branch, Mississippi, one day when a young woman came up to me and said, "Mr. Bell, word on the floor is that there will be a layoff." Certainly I had to show great discretion in how I answered that, especially since we had not made any final decisions.

"You know, these are tough times, and certainly we would be remiss if we didn't think through how best to run the company so that we have a company left after going through a recession," I explained. "I can tell you that we've had discussions about cutbacks and layoffs, but nothing has been finalized."

She took a deep breath and quietly asked another question. "Do you know how poor we are?"

Then and there, she had my undivided attention.

"If you lay us off, even for just a day, we won't be back," she said. "We'll have to find work somewhere else in Mississippi. We don't have anything."

Later that day, I visited the local gas station and convenience store. For a while, I sat and watched people come and go, and I reflected heavily on what that young, brave, humble woman had said to me. You see, we only have an opportunity to manage things for a moment in time. It is our responsibility to care for and nurture all that has been entrusted to us. A renewed desire to help our team of employees emerged.

The next day, I told management to figure out a plan that did not require anybody getting laid off. "That's impossible," they said, but I wasn't willing to give up.

Soon, we came up with a plan. We started by asking if anyone wanted to take a voluntary, extended vacation. Perhaps they wanted to work on a project or spend time with family. Sure enough, we had some takers.

Then, instead of laying off some employees outright, we took the remaining hours and divided them equally among our entire team. In the end, everyone had something to do and everyone got a check each week.

I truly believe God sent that woman to me so I could better understand what stewardship is all about. God calls all of us to be good stewards, but in this case, I was looking primarily at the big picture. As it turns out, the concept of stewardship is a lot more far-reaching than that. Sure, I was responsible for keeping our budget in line, but as a leader, I was also responsible for taking care of our people. Each of them was precious in God's eyes. To be good stewards of God's capital, we must remember to take good care of the company as a whole, but also the individual people who are the heart and soul of the company.

But who am I, and who are my people, that we should be able to give as generously as this? Everything comes from you, and we

have given you only what comes from your hand."

1 Chronicles 29:14, NIV

Rick Hawks, my pastor at The Chapel in Fort Wayne, Ind., once delivered a sermon based on this scripture. His key points were:

All wealth belongs to God

All wealth comes from God

All wealth returns to God

All wealth given to God is a privilege

But Who Am I?

It is important to recognize that all the things we are asked to manage are absolutely not ours. We have them for a moment in time, and all God wants us to do is be a good steward until we pass the baton onto the next person.

Life Lesson/Points to Ponder

- When faced with trials or roadblocks in life, how can you resolve the issues at hand?
- How can you think "out of the box" in an effort to care for those who have been entrusted to you?

- When someone suggests a different approach are you defensive? Or, can you rise and consider other opinions?

- What is your **Next Best Step**?

Crunching Numbers

When I was a young executive in the late 1970s, I had a chance to attend some educational seminars by a man named Curt. He was one of the few individuals who could help the average person truly understand the financial relationships in business between the profit/loss statement and the balance sheet.

Curt was excellent with numbers. He loved considering the financial impact of different scenarios, which included tweaks to pricing, volume, and other cost situations. He had a very simple and well-documented approach, and he could illustrate the projected impact of each scenario on the long-term investments of a company.

Years later, I asked Curt to be on our staff. I wanted him to educate our team by sharing his fine-tuned approach. Sure enough, he taught all of us to be better stewards of God's capital.

What happens when you change a price or adjust the volume in a company as it relates to the capital, the machines, the inventory and the extension of credit?

Curt made us think, and he made the business real to us – much like Jesus would do in his simple examples of stewardship.

> **Each of you should use whatever gift you have received to serve others, as faithful stewards of God's grace in its various forms.**
>
> **1 Peter 4:10, NIV**

There are times in your life when you may be encouraged to discover your spiritual gifts. God wants you to take whatever gifts you have and use them to serve others. Curt had a gift for making the complex world of business management seem simple and straightforward. Other people, you and me included, have other gifts. Figure out what your gifts are, and use them. God wants us to be good and faithful servants, and in the context of God's kingdom, we have only a moment in time in which to use the gifts He has given to us. We should aspire to please Him with a never-ending focus on grace.

> **A good person leaves an inheritance for his children's children, but a sinner's wealth is stored up for the righteous.**
>
> **Proverbs 13:22, NIV**

Our inheritance, friends, isn't just about money. It's about sharing our love for Jesus. This is the Great Commission, and, ultimately, it's up to us to make sure our children and our children's children have learned God's love and grace. That's why we're here. That is our purpose. Pass it on!

Life Lesson/Points to Ponder

- What are your spiritual gifts? (1 Corinthians 12:4-11) How are you using them to further the kingdom?

- What are you doing to pass on God's love?

- What is your **Next Best Step**?

A quick recap of Principle 7: Be a Thoughtful Steward of God's Capital and Focus Carefully on Results.

Focus

Principle 8: Mine Your Opportunities: Are They Real? Can You Win? Is It Worth It?

> **My son, if you accept my words and store up my commands within you, turning your ear to wisdom and applying your heart to understanding – indeed, if you call out for insight and cry aloud for understanding, and if you look for it as for silver and search for it as for hidden treasure, then you will understand the fear of the Lord and find the knowledge of God.**
>
> **Proverbs 2:1-5, NIV**

> **Now listen, you who say, "Today or tomorrow we will go to this or that city, spend a year there, carry on business and make money." Why, you do not even know what will happen tomorrow. What is your**

life? You are a mist that appears for a little while and then vanishes. Instead, you ought to say, "If it is the Lord's will, we will live and do this or that."

James 4:13-15, NIV

A Time-Tested, Trusty Checklist

Principle 7 dealt with stewardship. Most of the time, we think of managing things or assets. This section has a stewardship overtone with the management of ideas.

It is important for us to call out for insight as we seek for the hidden treasure God has in store for us. You will better understand the fear (respect) of the Lord in finding true knowledge.

When we read the book of James, we learn that we really can't predict the future. Our destiny is not our own. Our Heavenly Father is in the driver's seat – but that rarely stops us from trying to find a roadmap.

In the early 70s, I attended a seminar by Schrello Associates, Inc. Attendees were given a checklist that has helped me take ideas and bring them to fruition. It's a framework for assessing risks, and it is commonly called the Schrello Screen. The checklist is a holistic and robust way to evaluate a broad range of opportunities. Put simply, you ask the following questions:

Is It Real?

Can You Win?

Is It Worth It?

I have used this approach in business and the not-for-profit world. I've even had an opportunity to use it in evaluating opportunities for my family. Throughout the years, I've discovered scriptures that emphasize each point.

Is It Real?

> **"Ask and it will be given to you; seek and you will find; knock and the door will be opened to you."**
>
> **Matthew 7:7, NIV**

Can you touch it? Feel it? Smell it? Delve deeper. Take the time to ask the hard questions. Is there a need/want for this idea, product or opportunity? In business, when we explore whether there is a market for a specific product, we're asking "Is it real?" Hopefully, the answer is, "Yes, I've got a real product and a real market." This will work just as well in a church or family environment.

Can You Win?

> **Each of you should use whatever gift you have received to serve others, as faithful**

stewards of God's grace in its various forms.

1 Peter 4:10

This isn't about winning a game or finishing first. It's about matching your strengths and capabilities to the opportunity at hand. It may be real, but perhaps you don't have the right strengths to move it forward. Can you look toward the future and see the idea becoming a success? How will others respond to it? If there's a way to take advantage of the benefits and fill a need, a want or a hurt, you can probably win. Can your team take advantage of this idea?

Is It Worth It?

> **"Suppose one of you wants to build a tower. Won't you first sit down and estimate the cost to see if you have enough money to complete it?"**
>
> **Luke 14:28, NIV**

Here – and only here – you must consider the economics and risks of your idea. Can you afford to make this happen? Will you get enough out of the idea, end product or opportunity to justify what you've invested? Can you live with the risks? Ultimately, your goal will be to make sure that whatever idea you are considering aligns with your long-term vision.

Life Lesson/Points to Ponder

- What ideas has the Holy Spirit given you that you need to consider?
- Do you take the opportunity to celebrate when your ideas/projects come to fruition?
- What is your **Next Best Step**?

Try … And Then Try Again

Early in my career I met a creative inventor from Dallas, Texas. He had come up with an invention called an Untended Meal Dispenser, and he thought the speedy system would be a perfect addition to the silos where military personnel were tending our missiles. At the time, I was involved with developing foodservice systems for the U.S. Army, and this invention would give the troops a way to heat food quickly. We went ahead and built one, but sadly, the project fizzled.

Several years later I was speaking with Don on the phone, and I asked whatever happened to that machine.

"You'll never guess," he said. "I repackaged the device in a little box, and we're going to be able to make fried chicken like the fast food industry produces." It seemed as though he was on to something, so I flew to Dallas. It definitely had potential, but there was no way to manufacture it in those days.

Still, we didn't give up.

Years later Don created an even better model, and it solved a big problem. With this new oven, restaurants could cook a pizza in about five minutes, drastically reducing the amount of time their hungry customers needed to wait on a busy Friday night.

Soon, we were receiving orders from Pizza Hut and other restaurants across the country that wanted to decrease the amount of time it took to make pizzas and hot sandwiches. Today, you can go anywhere in the world and enjoy piping hot food because of the Impinger oven.

Do you have an idea you're trying to get off the ground? With God's help, you ask …

Is It Real?

Can You Win?

Is It Worth It?

It's no coincidence that this strikes a remarkable parallel to God's love for us. He gave us Jesus. Is being a Christ-follower real? Can we win, and is it worth it? If the reward is eternal life with Christ, you tell me.

> **Fight the good fight of the faith. Take hold of the eternal life to which you were called when you made your good confession in the presence of many witnesses.**
>
> **1 Timothy 6:12, NIV**

Life Lesson/Points to Ponder

- Sometimes when we start a project it turns out quite different than our initial idea. How do you know when you need to shift course?
- We are called to fight the good fight. What's your good fight? How recently have you stated your 'fight' to a friend or a family member?
- What is your **Next Best Step**?

A Different Spin on Seeking God's Wisdom

Rev. Robert H. Schuller of the Crystal Cathedral in Garden Grove, Calif., once gave a lecture in which he explained a very creative four-step process. It can be used to evaluate opportunities, giving focus to your ideas. In meditating over this process, I knew it was more than just another checklist. It was God-inspired. I have since added Scriptures that have spoken to me.

Step 1: DRIFT

> **Dear friends, do not believe every spirit, but test the spirits to see whether they are from God, because many false prophets have gone out into the world.**
>
> **1 John 4:1, NIV**

There are thousands and thousands of ideas that DRIFT into your brain each day. Some are good. Others, perhaps, don't have what it takes to get off the ground.

Step 2: SIFT

> **If any of you lacks wisdom, you should ask God, who gives generously to all without finding fault, and it will be given to you.**
> **James 1:5, NIV**

How do you figure out which ideas are the good ones? You SIFT by asking a few hard questions. Is this idea a great thing for my company, my church, or my family? Does this idea fill a need? Is there anybody else doing anything about it?

Step 3: LIFT

> **But test them all; hold on to what is good.**
> **1 Thessalonians 5:21, NIV**

Next you LIFT the idea. You find a way to turn your simple idea into an actionable plan. This is where you shift from the dreaming stage to the doing stage. Pray about it.

Step 4: GIFT

> **"Give, and it will be given to you. A good measure, pressed down, shaken together and running over, will be poured into your**

> **lap. For with the measure you use, it will be measured to you."**
>
> **Luke 6:38, NIV**

Finally, as the project or idea comes to fruition, you celebrate the GIFT that it has become and you share it with others and give it to God.

Life Lesson/Points to Ponder

- As Robert H. Schuller asked, what plans would you have on the drawing board if you knew it would not fail? Answer this question and apply the four step process to find out if it's worth it.

- When you are pondering new ideas, who are your trusted partners that can help you think through the process?

- What is your **Next Best Step**?

A quick recap of Principle 8: Mine Your Opportunities: Are They Real? Can You Win? Is It Worth It?

Peace

Principle 9: Be Still, Listen and Pray

> **For the Lord gives wisdom; from his mouth come knowledge and understanding. He holds success in store for the upright, he is a shield to those whose walk is blameless, for he guards the course of the just and protects the way of his faithful ones. Then you will understand what is right and just and fair – every good path.**
>
> **Proverbs 2:6-9, NIV**

> **'Call to me and I will answer you and tell you great and unsearchable things you do not know.'**
>
> **Jeremiah 33:3, NIV**

Do You Trust Me?

It was a very dark time in my life. At first, I thought I was depressed. We were in the midst of a national recession, and business was tough. Naturally, I was struggling to cope with the pressure.

Throughout the years, I had been through plenty of ups and downs. This time, however, the valley seemed especially deep and dark. I couldn't quite come to terms with everything that was going on. I was even having a hard time sleeping.

> **Praise be to the God and Father of our Lord Jesus Christ, the Father of compassion and the God of all comfort, who comforts us in all our troubles, so that we can comfort those in any trouble with the comfort we ourselves receive from God.**
>
> **2 Corinthians 1:3-4, NIV**

At church the next Sunday, I found myself talking to the man who was in charge of pastoral care. He suggested I make an appointment with someone who specialized in Christian counseling. I was not a new Christian, but despite my deep faith and my years of religious service, I was really struggling.

When I arrived, the counselor wasted little time. "Why are you here?" he asked.

I explained the struggles I was facing in life and business, and I suggested that I might be depressed.

"Let's find out," he said. He then proceeded to put me through a series of tests unlike anything I'd ever seen or experienced before, and the results were startling:

"You're not depressed," he said. "You don't trust God."

I'm a man of faith, a student of the Bible!

The counselor did not back down. "You don't trust God in the valley."

He began to explain how the brain and emotions work.

The counselor then asked me to share some memories and significant events in my life – as far back as when I was just five years old. God had been there the entire time. I just hadn't recognized it or given Him credit at those particular times in my life.

The counselor did another assessment that would tell us just how close I was with God and determine how well I could communicate with Him. It would also identify the disciple I am most like. This insight was fascinating. As it turns out, my temperament and leadership style are very similar to those of the disciple John, although I share some similarities with James and Phillip, too. Overall, I scored very high in the areas that indicated I could communicate with God.

Despite these revelations, my depression and anxiety were still very much a part of my life. I needed to learn how to control these things, which most often reared their ugly heads at times when I didn't trust God.

What's the fix? Surely there's a pill or a treatment that will help me get back on track.

"You have to be patient," the counselor said. "We're going to get you back into the Word, and you're going to deepen your relationship with God. Focus on a daily routine and try to discover the secrets of heaven. Wait upon the Lord. Meditate. Learn about absolute surrender. Quit performing for the praise of man. You only have to dance to one drummer, the applause of One."

> **If any of you lacks wisdom, you should ask God, who gives generously to all without finding fault, and it will be given to you."**
>
> **James 1:5, NIV**

Next Best Step

God was breaking me down. I didn't have a faith issue, I had a trust issue. God wanted my energy and my will, and I wasn't giving it to Him. I found some clarity in the fact that I had always been a people person. I thrive on others' energy, and helping them gives me great joy. It was time for me to focus more on *human being* and less on *human doing*.

After several sessions, the counselor said I didn't need to see him anymore. Before I left, he asked me one last question: "Would you like to learn to pray unceasingly?"

"Can't do that," I said. "It's impossible. That's a Biblical concept."

He proceeded to explain what he meant. Then, he told me to write down a simple question. *What does God want me to do next?*

"Do this … and then pray," he said. "Soon, you will begin to see God in ways you've never seen before."

This question – and the process of praying about it – ultimately became a personal motto for me. What is your ***Next Best Step***?

> **Rejoice evermore. Pray without ceasing. In every thing give thanks: for this is the will of God in Christ Jesus concerning you.**
> **1 Thessalonians 5:16-18, KJV**

My counselor reminded me that I'd have to stop and refocus on God over and over again throughout each day. Be careful not to get so wrapped up in little decisions that you lose sight of the bigger picture, he said. *I have to get in the shower. I'm late for my breakfast meeting. I have to take this urgent call.* No. Stop and refocus. Think about what God wants you to do next.

Christian evangelist and teacher Oswald Chambers said, "The toughest work in life is prayer." It's not easy to submit to God, it's not easy to glorify Him. It's not easy to say I'm going to listen.

> **Very truly I tell you, whoever believes in me will do the works I have been doing, and they will do even greater things than**

> **these, because I am going to the Father. And I will do whatever you ask in my name, so that the Father may be glorified in the Son. You may ask me for anything in my name, and I will do it.**
>
> **John 14:12-14, NIV**

Asking God for direction in your life is a matter of trust. When you find yourself in the midst of troubled waters – literally or figuratively – it's important to have faith in God.

Think of the time Jesus' disciples were caught in a rough storm in Matthew 14:22-33. The disciples were afraid, but eventually they looked up and saw Jesus walking toward them on the water. Peter tried to do the same, but when he heard the wind and saw the stormy seas, he lost faith and called to Jesus as he began to sink. Jesus grabbed him and pulled him to safety.

No matter what is going on in our lives, we have the opportunity to focus on Christ. When we do this, the circumstances pertaining to the situation get a little fuzzy and don't seem to matter as much. But when we focus on the circumstances of the situation, it's Christ that seems fuzzy.

Duke basketball coach Mike Krzyzewski has a similar philosophy. He tells his athletes to focus on the next play, no matter what. Win or lose: next play. Score a basket or turn over the ball: next play.

That's exactly what God wants us to do – pray for direction as we focus on our next play. When we pause to ask the question, we're opening our hearts to God's direction. It's a practical way to make Jesus Lord of your life. You allow Him to direct your small steps which ultimately pave a path toward big decisions.

So, what is your **Next Best Step**? Soon, you will begin to see God in ways you've never seen before.

Life Lesson/Points to Ponder

- Think about a time when you felt separated from God because of a difficult time you were going through? Was it easier to go through this all on your own or did you need to lean on God to feel the burden lift?

- Do you think it's possible to pray unceasingly? How did you learn to pray?

- What is your **Next Best Step**?

Learning to Listen

When our son Jim was eight years old, he got very sick. He had gotten a mosquito bite during the Labor Day weekend, and an infection from the bite caused his brain to swell. He was admitted to the hospital, and we soon learned that this was not an isolated case. There were five other children at the hospital with the same symptoms, and we knew that something wasn't right.

The Center for Disease Control later confirmed that some animal had come into contact with a bird, which in turn had come into contact with mosquitoes in this part of Indiana. Many children were being diagnosed with viral encephalitis.

Jim recovered from the encephalitis, but about six months later, he got sick again. This time, we were preparing for a spring break trip to Disney World. We weren't sure exactly what was wrong, but Jim's doctor prescribed some medications and told us we were free to travel.

While in Florida we stayed with some friends. Jim clearly wasn't well. At one point he doubled over in extreme pain. We took him to a doctor in Florida, and he said Jim was well enough to go to Disney World the following day and well enough to travel home.

Unfortunately, things didn't work out as we'd hoped. When we arrived at Disney World the following morning, we eagerly made our way to stand in line for our first ride. Moments later, Jim doubled over once again. We carried him out of the park and flew home, still uncertain about what was wrong.

Upon returning to Fort Wayne, we checked Jim into the hospital. Our doctor said he was unsure of Jim's diagnosis, but one possibility was Crohn's Disease. Unfortunately, the doctor said the hospital in Fort Wayne was not equipped with the right kind of X-ray equipment at that time.

I was in my mid-30s, and I had all the wisdom I needed -- or so I thought. I said to my wife, "We're going to Mayo."

Later, our doctor suggested Riley Hospital for Children in Indianapolis. At the time, we weren't familiar with Riley, and we were determined to seek the best medical help we could find. It didn't seem possible that Riley could compare with the highly-regarded Mayo Clinic, so I dismissed the suggestion.

I called Mayo and spoke with the head of pediatric gastroenterology. He listened to me describe Jim's symptoms and said, "Yes, Sir. Bring your son." Before we left, I looked at my wife and said, "You know, I might as well call this doctor in Indy, just to confirm he's the wrong one."

I called Riley and asked to speak with Dr. Fitzgerald. His nurse answered and told me he'd just left the building, but she could see him outside. She asked me to wait while she called to him through the window. Dr. Fitzgerald turned around and came back in to take my call, huffing and puffing a bit from hurrying back into the building.

I told him what was going on, and he said, "I don't know what's wrong with your son. Just go back to your room and pray." **Next Best Step**. God was working through Dr. Fitzgerald.

His willingness to take my call and his suggestion to pray struck me. I hung up the phone, and Pat and I prayed together. We prayed for guidance, asking God where we might possibly receive the best care for Jim.

> **In the same way, the Spirit helps us in our weakness. We do not know what we ought to pray for, but the Spirit himself intercedes for us through wordless groans. And he who searches our hearts knows the mind of the Spirit, because the Spirit intercedes for God's people in accordance with the will of God.**
>
> **Romans 8:26-27, NIV**

A few minutes later, I looked at my wife and said, "Hon, I think we need to go to Indy. I just have a feeling that this is what God is telling us to do."

So, instead of heading to Mayo Clinic, we packed up the car and drove to Indianapolis. There was a family center on the floor, and we gathered for a meal with other families whose children were also patients at the hospital. While we were eating, someone tapped my shoulder. It was Dr. Fitzgerald. "I've been studying your son's X-rays, and he has Crohn's Disease," he said. "I'm extremely familiar with Crohn's, as I am the chief pediatric advisor to Mayo Clinic on this disease."

There's no question in my mind that God had directed us to Riley Hospital in Indianapolis. Finding Dr. Fitzgerald was no random occurrence.

Certainly all the wisdom I had as a CEO meant nothing. God knew what we needed, and God answered our prayer. Our world turned 180 degrees in a matter of seconds. We found ourselves heading south to a small, lesser known hospital instead of heading north to a highly-regarded, world-renowned medical facility – yet, we received the very best care from the most experienced doctor in his field.

Prayerfully consider your **Next Best Step**, and give it all to God.

> **But when you pray, go into your room, close the door and pray to your Father, who is unseen. Then your Father, who sees what is done in secret, will reward you.**
>
> **Matthew 6:6, NIV**

Dr. Fitzgerald treated Jim for eight years. We truly let go and let God. Jim is now in his forties, and he has had significant trials and tribulations in his three-decade journey with Crohn's, but we are immensely thankful for the care he received at the time of his diagnosis and in the following years.

When facing times of trial, I encourage all of you to say, "What is my **Next Best Step**?" Train yourself to pray unceasingly, glorifying God in all you say and do.

> **Do not be anxious about anything, but in every situation, by prayer and petition, with thanksgiving, present your requests to God.**
> **Philippians 4:6, NIV**

Life Lesson/Points to Ponder

- Think of a time when you reacted quickly and then of a time when you listened, took time and then reacted? What action worked best for you?

- Share a time when prayer led you to do something that may not have made perfect sense at the time. How did God answer?

- What is your **Next Best Step**?

A quick recap of Principle 9: Be Still, Listen and Pray.

Risk

Principle 10: Don't Take It Easy, Take a Risk for God and Serve Others With Boldness

> **Cast thy bread upon the waters: for thou shalt find it after many days.**
>
> **Ecclesiastes 11:1, KJV**

The Great Commission

> **Therefore go and make disciples of all nations, baptizing them in the name of the Father and of the Son and of the Holy Spirit.**
>
> **Matthew 28:19, NIV**

Enjoy Life by Taking Risks

The Rev. Gary Skeeters, who became a pastor after a successful business career, once gave a sermon called "Bread Upon the Waters." The sermon, based on Ecclesiastes 11:1-6, has become central in my work as a business advisor. Sometimes, I call it the "Return on Investment Sermonette," and I use it often for business closings.

> **Cast thy bread upon the waters: for though shalt find it after many days. Give a portion to seven, and also to eight; for thou knowest not what evil shall be upon the earth. If the clouds be full of rain, they empty themselves upon the earth: and if the tree fall toward the south or toward the north, in the place where the tree falleth, there it shall be. He that observeth the wind shall not sow; and he that regardeth the clouds shall not reap. As thou knowest not what is the way of the spirit, nor how the bones do grow in the womb of her that is with child: even so thou knowest not the works of God who maketh all. In the morning sow thy seed, and in the evening withhold not thine hand: for thou knowest not whether shall prosper, either this or that, or whether they both shall be alike good.**
>
> **Ecclesiastes 11:1-6, KJV**

Cast thy bread upon the waters. In other words, we must put ourselves out there – in life and in business – by taking risks.

Give a portion to seven, and also to eight. For Solomon, this meant having seven or eight ships, because there was no way to know what would happen to them. One ship might sink, another might burn. A third, perhaps, would make money.

Today, investors and stock brokers use a similar approach. One particular stock may turn out to be a bad investment, but if you have a diversified portfolio, there's a good chance a few others will do well.

To build deeper relationships with people, I often use the following six points to explain further the lessons found in Ecclesiastes 11:1-6:

- **Take Risks**
- **Diversify**
- **Be Active**
- **Be Bold**
- **Celebrate**
- **Be Joyful**

My friend and mentor Mitch Kruse said, "Relationships are more important than remuneration, and people are more important than profit. When you have the first, the second takes care of itself."

Therefore, in taking risks and demonstrating God's unconditional love, we put our investment in people first.

Servant leaders need to create an environment that encourages unconditional love.

Toward the end of Ecclesiastes, Solomon gives us his bottom line:

Now all has been heard; here is the conclusion of the matter: Fear God and keep his commandments, for this is the duty of all mankind.

Ecclesiastes 12:13, NIV

When I read this verse, I believe the word 'fear' is intended to mean 'respect.' The goal is to honor God from a place of love and respect.

Life Lesson/Points to Ponder

- In what areas of your life do you need to be more bold?
- What are the characteristics of leaders who have unconditional love?
- What is your **Next Best Step**?

When a Small Yes Becomes a BIG YES

I received a call from a pastor at a very large church in town. He told me that many members of his congregation worked in the business I was managing and they were praying for my success. He asked if I would speak to a Sunday School class in the fall. I said sure. It should not be too difficult to address a small group.

When I arrived, I realized that wasn't exactly the case.

Instead of speaking to a Sunday School class, I was to lead an evening worship service, and the place was packed. Several radio stations and a live band were present. I was facing a much bigger challenge than what I'd originally signed up for.

> **And pray in the Spirit on all occasions with all kinds of prayers and requests. With this in mind, be alert and always keep on praying for all the Lord's people. Pray also for me, that whenever I speak, words may be given me so that I will fearlessly make known the mystery of the gospel, for which I am an ambassador in chains. Pray that I may declare it fearlessly, as I should.**
>
> **Ephesians 6:18-20, NIV**

After sharing some miraculous stories with those in attendance, I was asked to pray for the group at large. Many people who came forward received or renewed their commitment to Christ. That evening, when I returned home, my phone started to ring – calls from people I hadn't heard from in years from different parts of Indiana. They had heard the radio broadcast. A few days later, I got copies of letters from people saying they'd been at rock bottom but had a renewed sense of faith because of what I'd shared. Suicides were prevented. You just never know when something you say or something you do will impact someone else's life.

Life Lesson/Points to Ponder

- How are you satisfying the expectations of God? Do you see your role changing in one, five or ten years?

- Understanding that life is short and that we are only here for a moment. What are you doing to further the kingdom of God?

- What is your **Next Best Step**?

A Surprise Lesson

At age 60, I decided to go back to school. We were in a recession, and the services my company offered were not needed or working properly. I had read a book that convinced me I wasn't using the best approach, and I wanted to hone my skills.

A lot of my buddies told me I was crazy. They said I could teach the classes I was taking, but I knew that becoming a Certified Business Exit Planner was my **Next Best Step**.

I committed to a program of study, which led to a weeklong series of about 15 major lectures by professors and top industry consultants. When I arrived, it was easy to see I was the oldest person in the class.

The first night I went to dinner with a couple of guys whom I met in class. *Was I too old to be here?* While we ate, I received an alarming call: My son Jim was in the emergency room. Sadly, this was a common occurrence, as Jim has been dealing with Crohn's disease for most of his life. *I'm three hours away. I should forget all this and head home to be with Jim.*

I called my son right away, but he insisted that I stay in Chicago. "It's okay, Dad. Stay in school."

I teared up, and my fellow classmates kindly listened as I explained the situation. They were so kind and supportive.

We finished our meal, and left to explore downtown Chicago. My mind was elsewhere, though. In fact, I was still toying with the idea of driving home. As the night progressed, however, I began to ease up. Before I knew it, we were all laughing and joking as we walked downtown.

A man approached. "Looks like you're having fun," he said. We were about to keep walking, but then he asked us to buy him a meal.

I paused. "If you had enough money, where would you eat tonight?" I asked.

"There's a McDonald's a few blocks away," he said.

"All right, let's go."

As we walked to the fast food restaurant, I asked the man if he was a believer. He told me a story about his mom, and he shared how he learned about God. When we arrived, I told the man to order plenty of food – enough that he'd have something to eat the following day, as well.

"Are you sure?" he asked, over and over again.

I was sure.

If anyone has material possessions and sees a brother or a sister in need but has no pity

on them, how can the love of God be in that person?

1 John 3:17, NIV

Meeting that man on the street wasn't an accident. Sharing a meal with him was far more valuable than handing him a couple of wrinkled dollar bills. I helped him … but as it turns out, he helped me too. We talked, and in the course of our conversation, I was able to put my own situation in perspective.

In hindsight, it seems pretty clear that God was taking care of me that night. He saw to it that I'd be with Christian men when I received the news about my son being in the hospital. The men prayed for me, and they prayed for Jim.

And then God provided clarity and understanding through my encounter with the man who asked for money to buy food. In one short block, I stepped outside of my comfort zone, and I was able to change my perspective. I took a detour, but it turned out to be my ***Next Best Step***.

Take a risk for God and others.

Commit to the Lord whatever you do, and he will establish your plans."

Proverbs 16:3, NIV

When my weeklong class came to an end, I asked for permission to address the class. I read Ecclesiastes 11:1-6, the same sermonette from "Enjoy Life By Taking Risks." I encouraged everyone there to take risks for their clients and risks for God.

Looking in the rearview mirror, I can see that I was in Chicago to hone my own skills ... but also to help others in their own journey. I was exactly where I was supposed to be all along.

Becoming a Certified Exit Planner has given me the unique opportunity to help people at a critical time in their lives. Recently, I was named one of five Master Mentors by the Exit Planning Institute, and I consider that a true honor.

Each and every day, God wants us to take risks.

> **Therefore go and make disciples of all nations, baptizing them in the name of the Father and of the Son and of the Holy Spirit.**
>
> **Matthew 28:19, NIV**

Matthew 28:19 is commonly called The Great Commission. To me, the emphasis is on the verb "go." In carrying out The Great Commission, God gives us a way to prepare for each day of our lives by putting on the full armor of God. That preparation is best summarized in the following Scripture:

> **Stand firm then, with the belt of truth buckled around your waist, with the breastplate of righteousness in place, and with your feet fitted with the readiness that**

> **comes from the gospel of peace. In addition to all this, take up the shield of faith with which you can extinguish all the flaming arrows of the evil one. Take the helmet of salvation and the sword of the Spirit, which is the word of God.**
>
> **Ephesians 6:14-17, NIV**

Life Lesson/Points to Ponder

- As you interact with others, how do you support them in their quest to stand firm?

- Do you publicly Glorify the name of God?

- What is your **Next Best Step**?

A quick recap of Principle 10: Don't Take It Easy, Take a Risk for God and Serve Others With Boldness.

Servant LeaderShip Wisdom Mission

As you move forward in your own journey,
consider these words:

Servant Leaders have a loving heart while creating a culture to inspire others to strive for excellence.
They focus on building trust and commitment to their vision
while pursuing their passions.
They are messengers of hope and joy with a steward's heart,
Seeking God's wisdom to determine their Next Best Step in carrying out The Great Commission.

TM

But those who hope in the Lord will renew their strength.
They will soar on wings like eagles;
they will run and not grow weary, they will walk and not be faint.
Isaiah 40:31

Life Lesson/Points to Ponder

- What aspect of the mission statement do you need to work on?
- Think about the Scripture and how it applies to the Servant LeaderShip Wisdom Mission?
- What is your **Next Best Step**?

Reflections

A fire is burning, and I'm quietly reflecting.

As I look back on my life and these 10 Principles, I see that relationships are what matter most.

The two relationships that have been cornerstones in my life are my relationship with Christ and my relationship with my wife. Both offer me unconditional love.

It is my hope that these principles, scriptures and illustrations will speak to you and help you build your relationship with God and those who matter most in your life.

Understanding that I can pray 24 hours a day, seven days a week has been a significant revelation for me. It serves as a reminder that I need to put on the full armor of God and seek His will every single day.

And, as I move forward, I don't have to have everything figured out. I simply need to take one step at a time.

The same goes for you. Figure out your **Next Best Step**, and you'll be just fine as you navigate your own journey.

Along the way, remember that relationships with those around you are sacred. Relationships are key to being a loving servant leader.

Finally, the precious times when I am focused on *being* rather than *doing* are more joy-filled than anything. It is in the silence before and after these moments – praying with somebody in a hospital, spending time with my grandchildren or listening to waves splash as I sit on the back of my boat – that I feel closest to God. My hope is renewed and my joy is overflowing.

Discover your **Next Best Step**.

Best,

Gord

Maximizing the Use of Discover Your Next Best Step: 10 Proven Principles of Servant LeaderShip Wisdom

Discover Your Next Best Step: 10 Proven Principles of Servant LeaderShip Wisdom is an investment in your staff, your colleagues and, yourself. As the book was being developed, the author viewed this collection of Principles in many different ways in order to best meet the needs of the audience. The book is beneficial in the following settings:

- Small group settings, such as Executive Leadership Teams, Bible studies or task-focused teams as they launch into a major assignment or project.

- Lunch and Learn sessions, in which a single Principle is reviewed and discussed each time a group meets over the course of several weeks or months. Alternatively, principles can be discussed on an as-needed basis, when more focus needs to be paid to the application of a single principle that aligns with a shared corporate or community goal.

- Large group settings, where your goal is to share the Principals with an entire team, church congregation or company. Time for small group discussion is still recommended.

- One-on-one studies, in which the information is shared with specific individual for specific reasons; such as a protégée who needs to tighten his or her alignment with a company philosophy, or with an employee or team member who needs direction in improving his or her relationships with colleagues or customers.

- Individual studies may also be helpful when new members join your executive team after you have finished this study and you need to accelerate their understanding of the Principles. When using this book with a single individual, it is often helpful for the leader to connect with the individual on a regular basis, possibly after each Principle.

General use of *Discover Your Next Best Step: 10 Proven Principles of Servant LeaderShip Wisdom:*

- Clarify the audience and goals for using this book.

- Determine your plan for sharing the Principles. Will you schedule a series of meetings in advance, or will you schedule meetings as needs arise?

- Always read the Principle in advance and allow time for personal reflection prior to facilitating a group with others.

- Be familiar with the scripture and its context in relation to the writing.

- Review the examples used in each principle, and then personalize your own understanding of the principle by reflecting on your own experiences.

- When planning small group discussions, consider your audience. Will you divide attendees by a common characteristic, allow attendees to choose their own groups or assign groups ahead of time?

- As groups discuss each principle, it is important to roam the room and pay attention to those who are having lively discussions, those who are resisting the discussion or those who re having ah-ha moments.

- After groups have had ample time to discuss each Principle, you may choose to bring the larger group back together. You may choose to invite someone from each small group to share the highlights of their discussion with the larger group.

- If you plan to meet with your team or group over a series of dates, always tee-up an overview of the next Principle so members have time to pre-think this topic. You might also consider beginning each new session with a quick response to the last Principle studied.

  Example: *At our last small group session, we discussed Principle 1. What other thoughts have occurred to you as you applied that Principle over the past week or month?*

Discover Your Next Best Step: 10 Proven Principles of Servant LeaderShip Wisdom can be used in a variety of ways to meet an array of goals. Use this book in a way that helps you and your team or small group members grow. Enjoy your time with *Discover Your Next Best Step: 10 Proven Principles of Servant LeaderShip Wisdom.* It has been written for you as much as for your use with others.

Blueprint for Significance in Christ™
Action Plan

Develop your own personal ***Blueprint for Significance in Christ*** vision. So what's your Vision?

____

____

____

____

____

Where are you in the journey?

____

____

____

____

____

What **Next Best Step** did you take away from the 10 Principles?

____

____

____

____

____

"Always ask God in prayer, "What should I do next?" and glorify Him."

– Dr. Dan Boen

So what is your **Next Best Step** when you leave here today?

____

____

____

____

____

____

Principle 1: Love God, Love and Serve Others, Pursue Your Passions

____

____

____

____

____

____

____

____

____

Jesus replied: 'Love the Lord your God with all your heart and with all your soul and with all your mind.'
This is the first and greatest commandment.
And the second is like it: 'Love your neighbor as yourself.'
All the Law and the Prophets hang on these two commandments.

MATTHEW 22:37-40, NIV

Principle 2: What is Your Vision? Where are You in the Journey? Listen Carefully

Where there is no vision, the people perish:
but he that keepeth the law, happy is he.

PROVERBS 29:18, KJV

Principle 3: Develop a Culture With People Who Are Humble, Wise, Want to Do Their Best and Have Fun

Walk with the wise and become wise,
for a companion of fools suffers harm.
PROVERBS 13:20, NIV

Principle 4: Nurture a Caring Attitude, Create a Sense of Trust

You will keep in perfect peace
those whose minds are steadfast,
because they trust in you.
Trust in the Lord forever,
for the Lord, the Lord himself, is the Rock eternal.

ISAIAH 26:3-4, NIV

Principle 5: Strive for Excellence in All You Do

Finally, brothers and sisters, whatever is true, whatever is noble, whatever is right, whatever is pure, whatever is lovely, whatever is admirable – if anything is excellent or praiseworthy – think about such things. Whatever you have learned or received or heard from me, or seen in me – put it into practice. And the God of peace will be with you.

PHILIPPIANS 4:8-9, NIV

Principle 6: Serve Others and Keep Your Commitments

But let your word be 'Yes, Yes,'' or 'No, No'; anything more than this comes from evil one.

MATTHEW 5:37, NRSV

Principle 7: Be a Thoughtful Steward of God's Capital and Focus Carefully on Results

The man who had received five bags of gold
brought the other five. 'Master,' he said, 'you entrusted me
with five bags of gld. See, I have gained five more.'
His master replied, 'Well done, good and faithful servant!
You have been faithful with a few things: I will put you in
charge of many things.
Come and share your master's happiness!"

MATTHEW 25:20-21, NIV

Principle 8: Mine Your Opportunities: Are They Real? Can You Win? Is It Worth It?

Now listen, you who say, 'Today or tomorrow we will go to this or that city, spend a year there, carry on business and make money.' Why, you do not even know what will happen tomorrow. What is your life?
You are a mist that appears for a little while
and then vanishes. Instead, you ought to say,
'If it is the Lord's will, we will live and do this or that.'"

JAMES 4: 13-15, NIV

Principle 9: Be Still, Listen and Pray

'Call to me and I will answer you and tell you great and unsearchable things you do not know.'

JEREMIAH 33:3, NIV

Principle 10: Don't Take It Easy, Take a Risk for God and Serve Others with Boldness

Therefore go and make disciples of all nations,
baptizing them in the name of the Father
and of the Son and of the Holy Spirit.

MATTHEW 28:19, NIV

Public Speaking

Gordon Bell is a gifted storyteller. His engaging speaking style quickly captivates a crowd, making audience members feel like they are sitting in the company of a longtime friend. Gordon speaks on a variety of topics, including:

- Servant LeaderShip Wisdom (for adults and youth)
- Succession and Exit Planning
- Corporate Growth

No matter the topic, Gordon will help members of his audience think big. He'll encourage everyone to open their hearts and minds to the power of the Holy Spirit, and he will emphasize the importance of unlocking the Servant Leader buried within each one of us.

Gordon would love to join you for your next men's or women's ministry event, youth event, church leadership conference, corporate meeting, or corporate conference.

To inquire about his availability, email him at gbell@themidlandgroup.net.

Upcoming Publications by Gordon D. Bell

Gordon Bell is currently working on two upcoming book projects.

The first, a 30-day devotional for middle and high school youth, is being coauthored by Larry Lance, executive director of Fort Wayne Youth for Christ.

The second will be a guide for business owners as they are getting started, looking to grow or finishing strong gracefully.

Order Additional Copies of
Discover Your Next Best Step:
10 Proven Principles of Servant LeaderShip Wisdom

Name: ______________________________

Address: ______________________________

City: ________________ State: ____________

ZIP: ________________ Phone: ____________

Email: ______________________________

Quantity Ordered: ______ x $22.95 = ____________

Credit Card type: (circle one) Visa MasterCard

Credit Card#: ______________________________

Expiration Date: ______________________________

Name on Card: ______________________________

Signature: ______________________________

Email to: gbell@themidlandgroup.net

Mail to: Discover Your Next Best Step
993 Chestnut Hills Parkway
Fort Wayne, IN 46814

Phone: (260) 625-5595

Order online at DiscoverYourNextBestStep.com